Florida Travel Guide

The Top 10 Highlights in Florida

Table of Contests

Introduction to Florida

The Sunshine State attracts millions of visitors every year, not only because of its gorgeous beaches and warm climate, but also for some of the largest theme parks and museums in the world. Thanks to its warm climate, Florida has become a popular vacation destination in the past decades, especially during winter season.

Florida is the most south-eastern state in the United States of America and its capital, Tallahassee is closer to the Cuban capital, Havana than Washington D.C. Though Miami is probably the most well know city in this state, Jacksonville is the largest one.

The Sunshine State has plenty of beautiful beaches perfect for any type of visitors, but this is not the only reason tourists love to spend their vacations here. This state also boasts some of the most famous theme parks in the world, but also incredible wilderness.

Florida was discovered by Spanish explorer Juan Ponce de Leon in 1513 who named this land "La Florida" (The Flowery Land), because of its lush fauna. About three centuries later, in 1845, Florida became a state in the USA. Because it's very close proximity to many Latin countries, including Cuba, and the Caribbean Islands, Florida also has a very eclectic mix of cultural influences.

The Sunshine State has a very large Hispanic community that blended with all the European influences this state received throughout its history. Moreover, the northern part of Florida was also shaped by the Southern culture that dominates the neighboring states.

All in all, Florida boasts an eclectic culture that can be spotted everywhere, from its cuisine, to its architecture and traditions.

This state is also a magnet for conservationists and outdoor enthusiasts who get to discover incredible animal species like crocodiles, alligators, manatees and panthers, as some species can only be found in these parts.

1. Miami

Miami metropolitan area is the largest one in Florida and the actual city of Miami is the most popular destination in the Sunshine State, not just for its glorious beaches, but also for its spectacular nightlife. Its reputation for warm, balmy weather makes this travel choice a perfect one no matter the time of the year.

The first thing any visitor should do is hit the beach. Whether you're in search for the most crowded beach with a party atmosphere 24/7 in South Beach, or a more secluded one for lazy afternoons in the northern part of the coast, Miami has all of them. The coast is on a coral reef across Biscayne Bay and that is why the actual beaches are very wide with natural sand.

Those who are more interested in water sports can practice snorkeling and scuba diving in order to discover the beautiful underwater world. The best place to admire the marine life is definitely in Coconut Grove neighborhood.

After taking in all the beautiful, relaxing beaches of Miami, the next logical step is to explore de real culture of this multiethnic city.

Miami is also renowned for its Art Deco architecture, which can be observed at every corner. The Art Deco District, officially known as the Miami Beach Architectural District, is the perfect place to discover the largest collection of '20 and '30 resort architecture in the United States of America.

Little Havana is another neighborhood that cannot be missed. This place becomes even more popular during winter when almost every week there's another festival. As the name says it, Little Havana has a strong Cuban influence that can be observed in the architecture, cuisine and most of all the people and the language. It is thought that this is the place where Spanglish la language (a mixture of English and Spanish) was born. Here, tourists also have the opportunity to see firsthand how cigars are being made, all the while enjoying some of the most delicious coffee in the world.

Since Miami's atmosphere is strongly influenced by Latin and Creole culture, it is no wonder that this city hosts some of the most popular and large music festivals in the world. There's no place better to discover this eclectic culture like one of these events, particularly the Calle Ocho Festival on the avenue with the same name.

Shopping in Miami is almost a religion and some of the most luxurious shops in the world can be found on Ocean Drive and Lincoln Road. Aventura Mall also attracts thousands of shoppers in search for luxury brands. Close to the downtown area of Miami there's the Design District, where tourists and locals alike will find the artistic soul of this city. The entire neighborhood is lined with art galleries and dealers, furniture showrooms and many high end jewelry and fashion stores.

The cuisine in Miami is reason enough to spend at least several days here. Professional chefs and foodies alike make actual pilgrimages to Miami in order to sample some of the most innovative menus in the world. An entire new cuisine was created here in the 60's called New World and it blends the Latin American and Caribbean traditions with skills used in European menus. This new cuisine is in a continuous change thanks to Asian, Latin and African influences.

2. Orlando

Though Orlando is a beautiful destination on its own, the largest theme parks who are housed here make this city such a popular choice among tourists everywhere. With places like Walt Disney World Resort, SeaWorld Orlando, Universal Orlando and even the Kennedy Space Center, Orlando can entertain for days even the most capricious visitor.

Though the main attractions in this city are the theme parks, Orlando has many other interesting places tourists should not miss. The main city of Orange County has several large gardens and parks, the most important being the arboretum managed by University of Central Florida. The botanical garden covers well over 30 hectares, boasts more than 600 species of plants and is the perfect place to spend a relaxing afternoon.

Orlando also has many museums from art galleries with vast collection, to the more unusual Ripley's Believe It or Not! Orlando Odditorium, where curious visitors can explore very strange but nonetheless interesting relics.

On the other hand, after discovering all Orlando has to offer, the next logical step would be the theme parks and the most famous one is none other than Walt Disney World. Millions of children and adults alike love to visit this ginormous resort every year. Opened in 1971, this theme park has become the largest and most popular one in the world. Though, when tourist travel to Orlando, their main focus is this theme park, Disney World is not exactly in the city's limits, but about 34 kilometers away.

Disney World is an actual resort that spreads over 27,000 acres and boasts four large parks, dozens of hotels, a camping area, and a residential one not to mention several golf courses. It takes more than just a day to cover the entire "world".

The actual park was designed by the famous cartoonist Walt Disney even though he died years before the resort was officially opened. Disney World has four main theme parks and two water parks. Magic Kingdom was the first one built and is mostly famous for the Cinderella Castle, a perfect replica of the one that appeared in the original movie. All the attractions are dedicated to fairy tales and the original Disney characters. Epcot is twice as large as Magic Kingdom and celebrates human achievements, featuring many technological innovations. The most popular landmark in this park is the Spaceship Earth. The third park is Disney's Hollywood Studios which features all the show-business elements of the world of Disney. Here visitors can discover what inspired Walt Disney to create all his beloved characters and, of course, the famous Sorcerer's Hat, one of the most popular attractions in the entire resort. The last theme park, also the largest one in the resort, is Disney's Animal Kingdom. Here visitors get to learn more about animal conservation and, of course, admire the main attraction of this park, The Tree of Life.

Two lesser popular attractions in this resort are the water parks, Typhoon Lagoon and Blizzard Beach. Both of them are opened only nine months a year but in different time periods so that visitors always have at least one water wonderland to explore.

Tourists who are fascinated by the underwater world cannot miss another one of Orlando's famous theme parks, SeaWorld Orlando. This is not just a theme park, but also a zoological one with thousands of marine species. SeaWorld offers visitors the opportunity to have close encounters with magnificent animals like dolphins, killer wales, sea lions and flamingo birds. Of course, there are many theme rides like the Manta, a facedown and head first roller coaster.

The entire park is divided in several parts called "seas", each with a unique feature, from the legend of Atlantis to the Arctic continent and the iconic Killer Whale Show at the Shamu Stadium.

Movie buffs must not miss the opportunity to discover the magical universe of movies and TV shows at Universal Orlando, another one of the main theme parks in Orlando. The resort features two main parks – Universal Studios Florida and Islands of Adventures, each with many attractions and live shows.

Universal Orlando opened its gates in 1990 and since it has become one of the most popular parks in the world. Universal Studios was the first one built and it features themed areas dedicated to some of the most popular movies in cinema's history, from *Ghostbusters*, *Jaws* and *Back to the Future* to the more recent *Harry Potter* series.

The second theme park, Island of Adventure, was opened almost a decade later and it features seven large islands dedicated to various adventures.   The most popular ones are those dedicated to Jurassic Park and Harry Potter's "wizarding world".

Space aficionados, who don't mind travelling a little over 80 kilometers away from the city of Orlando, can discover everything there is to know about the US space program and its legendary history. Here visitors can explore several museums, a rocket garden, an IAMX which features movies about the space program or they can take a bus tour of former shuttle preparation and launch facilities.

3. Palm Beach

Palm Beach is a magnet for daredevils who love to spend their vacations doing all sorts watersports. With less than 10,000 inhabitants, this town, which lies on a 26 kilometers long barrier island, is the epitome of the perfect summer vacation.

Though this city doesn't have many important touristic attractions, the beaches are reason enough to spend at least a few days by the Atlantic Ocean. The tropical climate makes Palm Beach the perfect gateway year-round, and many celebrities has chosen this location to build their winter retreats. So you can expect to have a run in with movie stars, designers or musicians.

The most popular watersports that visitors love to practice here are parasailing, snorkeling, kayaking and paddle boarding. However, some down time just lying on the beach or swimming in the ocean, it's not out of the question.

If you get tired of so much water and sunshine, Palm Beach boasts several interesting spots that can keep you busy. If you want to indulge in some shopping, you can take a trip through Worth Avenue, where all the high-end boutiques are located.

Architecture buffs must visit the Mar-a-Lago estate, built by American socialite Marjorie Merriweather Post. Nowadays the estate is owned by real-estate magnate Donald Trump who turned the building into a club.

4. Everglades National Park

One of the most interesting and beautiful national parks in North America, the Everglades are a true playground for animal lovers and outdoor enthusiasts. With more than 1.5 million acres, this is one of the largest parks in USA. Though it covers a massive piece of land, the park only protects about 20 percent of the actual Everglades in Florida.

Every year, this park is visited by over a million tourists in search for untouched wilderness. However, since the 19th century, this area has drastically changed thanks to an agricultural and urban development program, which seriously decreased the size of this park.

The most popular attraction of this area is definitely the wildlife. The Everglades hosts some of the most deadly species in the world, from alligators and crocodiles to Florida panthers. The park houses over 1,000 species of plants and collecting plants and animals in this area is strictly prohibited. What is more, 36 animals that are federally protected live in Everglades National Park, among them being the American, crocodile several types of sea turtles, West Indian manatee and the Florida panther. The latter is one of the most endangered species in the world.

The Everglades is a true paradise for any birdwatcher. The park also houses over 350 species of birds from glossy

17

ibises and egrets to herons and Cape Sable seaside sparrow, most of them also on the endangered list.

Though the park is opened year-round, the best time to see it is during dry season between December and April. During the rest of the time, some facilities may be closed or may have restricted hours, depending on the weather.

The Everglades National Park can be seen via one of the several trails that vary in difficulty. The most popular one is Anhinga Trail, a half-mile route that passes through a saw grass marsh where tourists can spot alligators, turtles and wading birds. Visitors can also choose Gumbo Limbo Trail, just as long, which loops around a canopy of hardwood hammocks.

The area is divided into four visitor centers, where tourists receive informational brochures and can admire different educational displays. These are the perfect places to start your adventure.

Very close to this national park, there's another natural treasure - The Ten Thousand Islands. The chain of islands and mangroves are just off the coast of Florida and are virtually inhabited. However they are very popular among conservationists, nature enthusiasts and canoeists and sea kayakers. Don't be fooled by the name – The Ten Thousands Islands are actually just several hundreds.

5. Fort Lauderdale

The city of Fort Lauderdale is also known as the Venice of the US because of its large canal system. Though it's not a large city, For Lauderdale is a very interesting vacation option thanks to its wide beaches and busy nightlife, as well as for its museums and parks.

The first thing that visitors do when they get to this city is hit the beach and enjoy the beautiful sand and warm waters perfect for swimming and paddle boarding. There are several beaches, that line the 40 kilometers long coast line, and every single one of them is a perfect spot for any type of tourists. Nature lovers can even spot turtles nesting on some of these areas and the spectacle of tiny turtles trying to get to the sea is truly mesmerizing.

This city is also a pristine shopping destination, with some of the most famous designer flagship stores and car dealers' showrooms. The best places to find upscale restaurants and shops are definitely on Las Olas Boulevard and at Galleria Mall. Hard-core shoppers cannot miss the Fort Lauderdale Swap Shop, the largest daily flea market in the world. Here you'll also find the largest drive-in theatre which boasts 14 screens.

The city also houses beautiful gardens and parks, all influenced by the lush wildlife just outside Fort Lauderdale, in the Everglades. The Secret Woods Nature Center has three communities alongside the New River: a laurel oak hammock, an inland freshwater maple wetland and a mangrove community along the river. Wildlife enthusiasts have the unique opportunity to discover rare and exotic species in a true topical paradise. The Flamingo Gardens is a sanctuary for injured and non-releasable animals and houses the one of largest collections of species like flamingos, peacocks, bobcats, bears, alligators and otters. The Botanical Garden has thousands of exotic, tropical and native plants, while the arboretum houses some of the largest trees in Florida.

For a fairytale like afternoon tourists have to stop by the Butterfly World. As its name says it, this park has over 10,000 multicolored butterflies. The actual experience is truly mesmerizing, and no matter the time you choose to visit, you'll be able to admire dozens of species at once. The best part of this entire experience – the beautiful insects will most likely land on you.

Those who are in the lookout for more cultural attractions can visit the Museum of Art, one of the most acclaimed art galleries in Florida, with more than 6,000 pieces. The Museum of Discovery and Science offers inquiring minds over 200 exciting exhibits, including live animal habitats, flight simulators and the largest living coral reef in captivity. The aerospace exhibit is the most popular one, especially among children, while the IMAX Theater has one of the biggest screens in the entire state of Florida.

Fort Lauderdale's night life is just as exciting. Locals and tourists alike gather at Las Olas Riverfront where they can dine at upscale restaurants or admire the luxurious yachts that are docked in the harbor.

6. Boca Raton

Another beautiful and exciting city in Florida, no too far from the Everglades, is Boca Raton. This is mainly a destination for tourists looking for down time at the beach or on the golf course. However, that doesn't mean Boca Raton doesn't have plenty of museums, clubs and shopping malls.

The shore in Boca Raton is a lot quieter and secluded then the rest of the coast, with large beaches perfect for swimming and snorkeling. On the eastern shore, by the Red Reef Park and South Inlet Park, snorkelers can reach a living reef without having to rent a boat. Boca Raton also has excellent golf courses, many of them right on the beach.

Tourists who want to get a taste of Asian culture can seek refuge in the Japanese Gardens and at the Morikami Museum. A century ago, a colony of Japanese immigrants, named Yamato Colony, tried to initiate here an agricultural community. Though their efforts were in vain, George Morikami, one of the immigrants who work for this program, donated 200 acres of land to celebrate this effort. The timeline of this program can be discovered at the museum that has its creator's name. The institution also hosts an array of cultural events, tea ceremonies and different classes.

Outdoor enthusiasts can discover the native wildlife in a 20 acres park along the coast, the Gumbo Limbo Environmental Complex. Here conservationists fight to preserve the beautiful landscape and many species of plants and animals. The park is named after a local tree and it features a museum with educational displays and live animals that can be admired up-close.

Another place that cannot be missed is the Sugar Sands Park. An enormous playground for children and their parents, this park features huge forts, jungle gyms, carrousels and many other rides. The recreational area also has an indoor gymnasium and a movie theater, so it will keep buy even the most energetic children.

7. Tampa

On the other side of the state, by the Gulf of Mexico, there's another city that cannot be missed. Tampa is one of the largest cities on the western coast of Florida and a very exciting travel destination. Just like most cities in Florida, Tampa has many beautiful beaches perfect for some relaxation, but they are not the only reason to spend time here.

Tampa is the ideal place to take a cruise from one of the fastest growing ports in USA. Also the city has a great variety of attractions like the one of the top 10 aquariums in the country, a very life-like dinosaur world and, of course, the always entertaining pier area.

The coast line of Tampa has award winning beaches with white sand and shallow waters, perfect for swimming and snorkeling. However, the Port of Tampa is where all the action takes place. This is one of the most popular ports from where millions of tourists take sail to exotic places.

Tampa offers tourists a wide variety of entertainment possibilities, from interesting museums and fascinating parks. The Florida Aquarium is one of the largest and most popular one in the country and offers curious visitors the chance to see up-close penguins, sharks, alligators, stingrays and many other marine species. What is more, those with enough courage can dive with sharks or swim among beautifully colored fishes.

The Lowry Park Zoo houses a couple of thousand animals in their natural habitat. Here tourists can explore several ecosystems like the Aquatic Center, Primate World, Safari Africa or Florida Manatee. Moreover, those who are interested in more... prehistoric species can always take a trip among thousands of year old dinosaurs in the fitly named park – Dinosaur World. Tourists can literally walk among these prehistoric creatures and discover authentic fossils.

Busch Gardens is another option for animal lovers to spend an afternoon. The park has more than 335 acres of African habitats filled with a wide variety of animals, but also some of the most exciting rides on this side of the state. Whether you want to try every single heart-stopping ride or get close to exotic and beautiful animals, Busch Gardens will keep you entertained for hours.

Don't forget about the Giraffe Ranch either, the place where you'll be able to pet and even play with the tall inhabitants of this beautiful place. The ranch perfectly replicates the African landscapes and houses some of the most popular animal species from the continent – giraffes, rhinoceros, pygmy hippopotamus, antelopes, zebra and ostrich. Exciting, isn't it?

Like most cities in Florida, Tampa has a large Latin community and the city's culture is strongly influenced by that aspect. The perfect place to discover this side of Tampa is Ybor City district. Named after its founder, cigar lord Vincente Martinez Ybor, this neighborhood has the oldest and most beautiful architecture in the city. In the 19th century Martinez Ybor built a cigar factory here, which quickly became the largest one in the world. Nowadays, the area features upscale restaurants, art galleries and boutiques.

8. Key West

Key West is a true playground for vacation makers who love to spend time in the sun, beachside. The city is actually an island a little over 100 kilometers from Cuba in the Gulf of Mexico. Actually Key West is a border of some sorts between the Atlantic Ocean and the Gulf of Mexico. The island has always been a destination for party seekers who are attracted by the artistic, laid-back scenery of this corner of the world.

Though the majority of tourists choose this destination for its busy nightlife and gorgeous beaches, Key West also has an historical district. The city is considered the southernmost town in the continental US and it's connected with the mainland by the Overseas Highway, an over 200 kilometers log highway that ends in Key West. The actual city is breath-taking, but even the drive there is impressive as the highway is mostly surrounded by water.

Key West is an exciting mix of Southern flavor, mellow lifestyle and strong Caribbean influences. This eclectic combination has been attracting people for the past two centuries, including Ernest Hemingway and Tennessee Williams, who found true inspiration on this island. The house where Hemingway lived while spending time in Key West is one of the most popular attraction on the island, mostly because the descendants of Hemingway's cats are still roaming the estate. Fun fact: all of them have extra toes, just like their ancestors. Tennessee Williams also had a house on the island, a small bungalow that is privately owned. However, that doesn't stop literary aficionados to pay their respects at the door of the famous playwright.

The main attraction of the island is the beautiful water and large beaches perfect for a laid-back vacation. Those in search for the perfect place for diving choose Key Largo Island where tourists can swim with dolphins and explore the living coral reef just a few kilometers off the shore.

The Old Town, the original Key West neighborhood, features classic bungalows and old houses which date back from late 19th century and early 20th century. The Old Town center is a true open-air museum for architecture buffs. Don't be surprised if you spot chickens walking freely on the streets of the city. The fowl inhabitant of this island have been roaming the streets freely for the past few decades so don't be surprised to see luxury cars stopping abruptly on the street so that a rooster can strut along the road.

Some curious can venture outside the island to the Dry Tortugas National Park. This park is only accessible by boat as the park is located 100 kilometers away from Key West on about 60 acres island in the Gulf of Mexico. Here tourists love to do discover the thousands of bird species that live here among the ruins of Fort Jefferson, a huge unfinished fortress, which is considered the largest masonry building in the Western Hemisphere.

9. Daytona Beach

Daytona Beach is mostly famous for two things – car racing and its beaches. It is less than 100 kilometers from the great city of Orlando, and houses NASCAR's headquarter, which means the city hosts many racing events throughout the year. Also, Daytona Beach is the favorite spring break destination for most American students.

Of course, as the city's name says it, Daytona Beach has more than 40 kilometers of great beaches, perfect for those epic spring breakers that swarm the city in March and April. Swimming and surfing are the main activities students love to do, apart from the lively nightlife this city is also famous for.

The boardwalk and pier is also a very popular spot in the city with beautiful retro buildings and fancy restaurants. The boardwalk is lined with fun rides for thrill seekers, like the Sandblaster Roller Coaster, or the more romantic Ferris wheel.

Daytona Beach is also known as "The World Center of Racing", which means millions of motorsports fans invade this city every year, especially during Daytona International Speedway Event. The Speedway has a 168,000 capacity and hosts different races with various cars, including go-carts, pickup trucks and motorcycles. The actual race track can be visited any time, depending on the races. Another widely popular race event is Daytona 500 which takes place on an actual boulevard in the city, fitly named International Speedway Boulevard. This avenue is lined with museums, pit stop demonstrations and racing simulators all dedicated to the number one sport in Daytona Beach.

This city also has a penchant for throwing exciting festivals. There at least one each month, but fall season is definitely the busiest one. From the Blues festival to Biketoberfest and the even funnier named, Turkey Run, all these events attract millions of tourists in search for a good time.

Those who are more interested in more cultural attractions also have plenty of options to choose from. They can spend time at the Art and Science Museum where they can discover more than 30,000 artefacts, including a giant complete sloth skeleton and a large exhibit of Cuban art. In fact this is one of the largest museums in the entire state of Florida.

For a more romantic trip, tourists can explore the shores of Ponce Inlet, a little town just outside Daytona, famous for its lighthouse. This is the tallest lighthouse in Florida and the second tallest one in the US (it's over 50 meter tall). The Ponce de Leon Inlet Lighthouse also houses a museum where curious visitors can discover this building's long history. However, the best part is the breathtaking view over the Atlantic Ocean that can be admired from the top of the lighthouse.

10. Fort Myers

At the beginning Fort Meyers was an actual fort, one of many built along the Caloosahatchee River against the Seminole Indians. Though it was destroyed by a hurricane during the 19th century, decades later, the site of Fort Myers was turned into a city, one of the largest ones in the area.

Most cities in Florida boast great beaches, and Fort Myers is no exception. Tourists love to fish, admire dolphin playing or simply swim in the gulf and discover the beautiful underwater world. The post popular spot is the Fort Myers Beach pier where visitors and locals alike spend time relaxing and basking in the Florida sun.

Fort Myers is also popular for two of its most famous inhabitants: Thomas Edison and Henry Ford. Both of them had winter homes here, which, after their death, became world-renowned museums. Edison bought a property in Fort Meyers in the 19th century that became his vacation home. A few decades later, Edison's good friend, Henry Ford bought the adjoining propriety which was also transformed into a winter retreat. After their deaths, both houses became propriety of the City of Fort Myers and were turned into a museum. Thus the Edison and Ford Winter Estates came to be.

The entire estate houses a museum and over 20 acres of gardens. Edison's Botanical Garden has over a thousand of plants from around the world, including a 120 meter tall banyan tree that was planted in the 20's. The estate also houses Edison's laboratory where he started working on a project that, after his death, lead to the discovery of rubber, but also the Henry Ford Inventions Museum.

Not too far from Fort Myers, tourists can discover one of the most beautiful islands off the coast of Florida - Sanibel Island. A barrier island, Sanibel is mostly famous for its incredible beaches and beautiful sea-shells.

Printed in Great Britain
by Amazon